At the
Shops

Paul Humphrey

Photography by Chris Fairclough

W
FRANKLIN WATTS
LONDON·SYDNEY

First published in 2005 by
Franklin Watts
96 Leonard Street
London EC2A 4XD

Franklin Watts Australia
Level 17/207 Kent Street
Sydney NSW 2000

© 2005 Franklin Watts

ISBN 0 7496 6178 X (hbk)
ISBN 0 7496 6190 9 (pbk)

Dewey classification number: 381'.1

A CIP catalogue record for this book is available
from the British Library.

Planning and production by Discovery Books Limited
Editor: Rachel Tisdale
Designer: Ian Winton
Photography: Chris Fairclough
Series advisors: Diana Bentley MA and Dee Reid MA
Fellows of Oxford Brookes University

The author, packager and publisher would like to thank the following
people for their participation in this book: Samiya and Lucsir Latif
and family; Focus Do-It-All and ASDA, Nottingham.

Printed in China

Contents

Dad and Samiya went shopping.

Shopping

Cheese
Milk
Eggs
Bread

Oranges
Carrots
Sugar

5

On the way to the shops, they saw Uncle Latif.

Please can you buy me some nails?

6

First, they went to the supermarket.

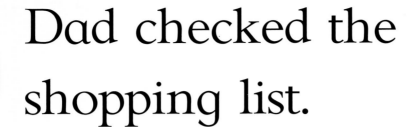

Dad checked the shopping list.

They went to the bread counter.

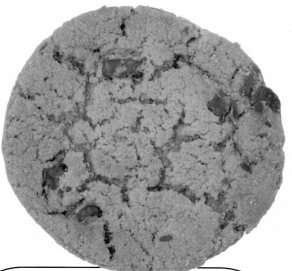

Can I have a cookie, please?

15

They finished
the shopping
and went to
pay at the
checkout.

ASDA
Price

Always LOW PRICES

ASDA STORES LTD.
WWW.ASDA.COM

HYSON GREEN,
ST. 4938 OP. 00000943 TE 17 TR. 06628
2222   000002719378   £0.99D
COOKIES 5PK 023211000034   £0.84D
ORANGES 1KG 0000027430001   £0.98D
CARROTS.   000002300350   £0.54D
WHT BAGUETTE 000002117238   £0.42D
BREAD   000002041536   £0.44D
BREAD   000002041536   £0.44D
CHUPA MAX   000008419655   £0.15V
S/P CHEDDAR 026058600170   £1.70D
S/PRICE EGGS 000002040846   £1.16D
WHOLEMEAL TN 023003000062   £0.62D
ASDA MILK   000002033216   £1.03D
MALTESERS   500015930825   £1.78V
SILVER SPOO 501006730150   £0.68D

                        £11.77
               TOTAL   £20.00
               CASH   £8.23
            CHANGE DUE

Dad took the bags out of the trolley. He loaded them into the car.

Next, they went to the hardware shop.

Samiya gave Uncle Latif his hammer ...

... and enjoyed
her cookie!

Word bank

Look back for these words and pictures.

Checkout

Cookie

Eggs

Hammer

Hardware shop

Nails

Shopping list

Supermarket

Trolley